# Reflections Off the Lake

## Poems on Life, Love and Democracy

# Books by Steven O. Ludd

Confronting the Politics of Gridlock
Revisiting the Founding Visions in Search of Solutions

Reflections Off the Lake
Poems on Life, Love and Democracy

Sherri

# Reflections OFF the Lake

## Poems on Life, Love and Democracy

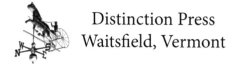

Highland
Lake
Winsted, CT.

Enjoy! 10/12/22

So Happy to
Connect with you!
Love
Maurice

# Steven O. Ludd

Distinction Press
Waitsfield, Vermont

Reflections Off the Lake
Poems on Life, Love and Democracy

Steven O. Ludd

Distinction Press
Waitsfield, Vermont 05673
distinctionpress.com

Watercolors©2000-2022Maurie Harrington
maurieharrington.com

Tradepaper ISBN 978-1-937667-29-0
Hardcover ISBN 978-1-937667-30-6

Library of Congress Control Number: 2022908656

# Dedication

For Those On the Journey To Freedom

# Acknowledgments

Without the support and expertise of these individuals, this book would not have been possible. I owe them a debt of gratitude that can not be fulfilled simply by saying thank you. But this is a beginning.

Kitty Werner's amazing skill at balancing verse and imagery created a text which will encourage the reader to think and dream at the same time. Her years of experience in publishing provided the necessary professional advice regarding structure and production essential for a seamless process from beginning to end. Her patience and straight-forward advice provided the guidance that most authors can only dream of acquiring.

Maurie Harrington's phenomenal artistic talents which appear both on the cover and throughout the book are both beautiful and powerful. Her scenic paintings, many of which are of Vermont's landscape, captured the essence of the poems and of the state that I love. I am humbled that she was willing to participate in this project.

Hank (Henry) Liebling, no stranger to the publication process and a citizen committed to the protection of democratic values both in America and throughout the world, constantly provided his insight and support for this book. His dedication to principles of good government and each citizen's responsibility in securing the values enshrined within our Constitution have never waivered across five decades. His support was invaluable.

The initial vision for this book simply would have languished and never been given birth if it was not for my son, Ian Sheldon Ludd. Having listened to many of the verses which appear in this book, he encouraged me to bring them out from the shadows into the light. May some of the verses also inspire others of his generation to continue their support for the defense of democracy throughout the world and be comforted by the beauty of our environment and the necessity of its protection.

As any spouse whose partner participates in the writing process can attest, communication can sometimes be complicated. But I have been fortunate to receive both understanding and constant support throughout this journey from my wife Oksana Mihaychuk Ludd. Whether the task was listening to a draft of a verse or simply providing the space for reflection, she was a partner in the process. I will be forever grateful.

# Contents

Messages From the Cavern Wall  9

Introduction  11
Incantations and Remembrance  12
A WARNING  15
Heroes  16
Boxes  17
"A Republic: If You Can Keep It"  18
A Deadly Mixture  20
Fear and Loathing  21
The Old Elm Tree  23
The Call  25
Staring Down the Bully  27
Resolve and Resist – Slava Ukraini  28
Don't Look Away  30
A Dream on the Train to Safety  31
A Conversation  33
And This Too Shall Pass  34
The Little Song Bird - (Amellia Anisovych)  35
On A Clear Day  36

Opening the Door  39

The Messenger  40
Last Night  42
Coming Thru to the Other Side  43
Questioning the Process  44
Trying to Find Balance  45
A Tribute to Thich Nhat Hanh  47
Free Will: A Suggestion  48
The Challenge  49
Thinking Aloud  50
Question Asked and Answered  52
Celebrate the Intangible  54
4 a.m.  55
The Unity of Opposites  56
Listening  57
Understanding the Danger  58
Modern Man  59
Centuries Have Past  60
Reflections Off the Lake  61
Choosing  62

## Nature's Reprieve, From Inside Looking Out   63

Thank You   64
From My Window   65
Wondering   66
No Regrets   67
On A Cold Winter's Morn   68
A Mountain Pond   69
Coming to an Understanding   73
A Breach of Contract   75
A New Addition to the Garden   76
Fly Fishing on the Battenkill   78
The Upper Hollow Road   79
An Ode to Vermont   80
Fall in the Woodlot   83
A Vermont Walk   84
Seasons   85
A Celebration   86
Sweet Expectations   87

## Memories: The Past, Present, and Future Converge   89

Memories   90
A moment in Time   91
A Christmas Gift   92
Alone   94
A love Lost   95
Sunrise   96
A Frequent Visitor   97
Augustus and Gratitude   98
Feeling   99
The Old School House   100
The Blue Spruce   102
The Ice Box   103
Grammy's Clock   105
His Time to Go   106
An Australian Visitor   108
The Christmas Cactus   109
A Place in Time   110
On To the Next Journey   112
Waiting   114
A Request   115

## About the Author   116

# Introduction

Poetry and prose, to some degree
Is a form of psychotherapy
Rooted in differing levels of creativity

It provides the writer with both an emotional
And intellectual outlet

The process is sometimes a subconscious communication
Placed in the random ether of others seeking connection.

It is akin to being placed in a darken room – reaching for a lamp
Fumbling sometimes in exasperation trying to find the switch
Only to stumble into a piece of furniture
Obstructing the path to the Light.

# Messages From
# the Cavern Wall

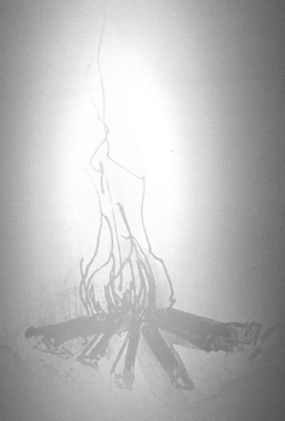

# Incantations and Remembrance

As they huddled close to the fire
Deep within the cave,
A nightly ritual of recounting stories passed down
From the Elders began.

They knew that these past events must be saved.
Each contained messages from times when cold and ice
Covered their ancestral lands. Before the great Flood.
When there was much sacrifice.

The stories were filled with advice on how to survive
The daily struggles against starvation
And the importance of insuring the Clan's protection
By making strong spears and clubs.

The stories, told by the oldest of the Clan, contained parables
Intended to be memorialized for future generations
Which is why the youngest of those circling the fire
Were always placed next to the Elders retelling the stories.

Even the most powerful of the community sat silently
Exhibiting great respect.
For they had also once heard the stories
Sitting close to their mother's breast.
They knew that their time was short
And if the tribe was to survive,
It was the young that must be taught
Both of the importance of strength
And respect for those who were not of the Clan
But who came in Peace.

In the second decade of the Twenty-first Century
After millennia have past
Why? Some would ask,
Is this relevant to the issues confronting humanity today?

Indeed, some of our most esteemed academics have presumptively
Cast aside any insight that may be gleaned from the so-called
"incantations" of prehistoric Man.

They would submit that "mankind has progressed
With the advent of social science."
Coupled with the technological innovations too numerous to
mention,
It is argued that to suggest that any insight which can be gleaned
from Messages
On the Cavern Walls is sheer intellectual blasphemy.

Having survived the so-called rigors of the Academy,
I humbly disagree.

Invasions of sovereign countries with the use of force
and the threat of nuclear destruction
The genocide of the "others" in countries across the globe
The growth of authoritarianism even in Democracies
Signal that homo sapiens still remain too often incapable of acting
rationally.
Gandhi once wrote that Western Civilization was "an interesting
concept".

Of course, suggesting that the hubris reflected in centuries of
European
Colonialization of the planet and its subsequent subjugation of
indigenous
People was certainly open to question as an example of civilized
action.

While Gandhi G's strategy of peaceful non-resistance to autocratic
rule in India
Achieved its initial goal of ending British colonization evolving in
to eventual Independence,
It came at a price.

Religious intolerance and political greed
Overwhelmed his historic efforts to build a nation on the concept
Of tolerance and peaceful co-existence. He did not succeed.

Today, one of the largest democracy's
Is still struggling with the impact of Partition
Of millions of its citizens
Based on their religion
Into two separate nations
Both competing for strips of land threatening each other with weapons
Of mass destruction.

This example is not intended to minimize the significance of the
teachings and actions
Of one of the world's greatest "seers" who offered those willing to open
their hearts
And minds to the importance of peace and tolerance.
But is offered to remind us all of the danger of failing to recognize the
ever presence
Of the dark forces in the world.

The messages of survival echoed within the cave
Told by the Elders millennia ago still resound in the Twenty-first
Century.
Survival of the Clan of homo sapiens is dependent upon accepting those
From outside the cave – but – who come in peace
And of the importance of standing in solidarity
Against those who market intolerance, subjugation, and hate.

# A WARNING

Deep within the cave
Lined across its walls
Appear messages from our past

Like the cries from a child lost from its mother
They are fearful calls from our ancient kinsmen.

Incantations of their moments in space.

Listen: "We are the tribe of Un.
We hunt the great beasts for meats and skins.
We come in peace. We shall survive.
Remember us."

Will we be remembered?

# HEROES

I was searching for heroes the other day
And what I found was quite disturbing I must say.
Neither wealth or status, power or privilege seemed to reveal
What I was looking for.

But, I thought, maybe physical beauty or adornment
Held the key to the door.

No. They are too ephemeral.
There must be something more.

Lost as I seemed to be in search for my heroes
To rescue me, I thought,
Who would come to save us all
From the hatred and vitriol
Produced by intolerance, corruption, and greed?

Then suddenly my quest was interrupted by some welcomed guests.
Above me I heard the chirping of a flock of Chickadees
Winging from tree to tree
Unencumbered by human insecurities.

They were a forgotten reminder of the universal truths
Which give birth to the creation of all that is good under Heaven:

Selfless kindness from those who have to those that don't;
A never-ending commitment to objective truth;
The ability to humbly admit mistaken opinion or action;
The need for individual and collective forgiveness and redemption.

This epiphany foretold the mistaken premise of my search for heroes.
It was an ill-faded venture, indeed.

There are no heroes who can save us and our Democracy.
We are the anchors who must steady the ship.
We the People.
The script has been written.

We must follow it.

# Boxes

Are you Left or are you Right?
Black, Asian, Hispanic, or White?
Old or young? Join the fight.

Male or female, short or tall
Fat or thin? That tells all.

What lurks within the box?

Hurry! A judgment must be made.
Your brand must be created.
No time to differentiate.
One size fits all.

But I recall a place in time
Where questions were asked.
That was the important task.
The reward was in the process
Not in channeling some pundit's blast.
We reveled in the journey
Not the destination.

It must have been my imagination.

# "A Republic: If You Can Keep It"

Locke wrote of "man in a state of nature."
He described the essentiality of liberty and its limits.
It was an important perspective for colonial Americans
As they roamed the wilderness searching for freedom
And a new life they could call their own.

Rousseau, Montesquieu, and de Tocqueville added their visions of
government
And the need for continual vigilance of private and public corruption
Sometimes created by a concentration of power and its seduction.

Heeding the warnings of these philosophers who came before,
Hamilton, Jefferson, and Madison also offered their perspectives
As they helped shape the contours of our Democracy.
Jefferson recognized the need for an "enlightened citizenry,"
Madison wrote of the necessity of constitutional government
Dependent upon institutional "checks" on "factions" in an attempt
To minimize tyranny from either the majority of the citizenry
Or the establishment of minority rule.
Hamilton was convinced that an "independent judiciary"
Was the answer to resolve governmental conflict.
But, it was Franklin who took his colleagues to school.

He reminded them that regardless of the newly crafted compact,
Its ultimate success was dependent upon the People

And their willingness to accept its precepts.

We had created a Republican form of government
Tied to a Constitution and ultimately a Bill of Rights.
It was the bi-product of Compromise
And of highly charged fights.

Our generation of Americans are now confronted with the question
Presented by Franklin: Can we keep it?
Will we preserve the Nation once perceived
Or fall to the forces of corruption and greed?

Lincoln asked the same question at Gettysburg:
"Can a nation conceived in liberty and dedicated to the proposition
That all men are created equal…long endure?"
The blood of hundred of thousands of citizens was spilled
In trying to answer the question.

Here is a suggestion: Reject Insurrection;
Turn out in great numbers in the next election;
Expose the autocrats who would destroy
The will of the majority
And demand the reinstitution of critical thinking in our schools
Thru the balanced study of our history as a People.
Both the good and the evil.

Our children will never forgive us if this is not done.
We owe them this sacrifice – at a minimum.

# A Deadly Mixture

The lid to the drum is fastened tight.
It is secure. No potential to spill or create a fight.
Not a word to challenge what is thought to be true
By those who have decided that they are Red or Blue.

No appreciation for the importance of nuance
No thinking out side of the Box.
No recognition that liberty cannot by preserved by anarchy.
Not a mention by some that wide economic disparities in our
Democracy
Has created social inequities which continue to go unaddressed.
Like a drum filled with explosive chemicals
Allegedly sealed tight. It is a recipe for a catastrophe.

All it takes is for those whose scared oath it is to oversee its safety
Is to slowly unseal the lid
And bring the mixture into the open
With objective debate and remedies
Before there is an explosion
Which will leave innocent citizens dead.

# Fear and Loathing

I awake some mornings with fear for humanity.
Reports of cruelty impacted upon the "others"
By some freshly minted dictator
Who has come to power through the use
Of military force.
Or, the emergence of self-aggrandizing grifters
Using division to grab power
With the help of citizens unable to see
The dangers being created to our Democracy.

The mass media's misuse of reporting "both sides" of our politics
Without objective journalistic analysis
Creates "false equivalences"
Leaving too many citizens trying to discover objective information
Not knowing where to turn.

Indeed, our politics has become so toxic, emboldened thru the use of
social media platforms,
That the current situation is now akin to children arguing on the
playground about some
Disagreement, ending in a fight – with the aggressor yelling in defense of
some unacceptable
Behavior – "Well, you did it to me first!"

Of course, there are answers to our current political and societal
differences,
And while suggestions have been offered by many,
There remains a fundamental observation that is at the core of resolving
our
Present collective insanity which is destroying our Democracy.
That is, while we are all entitled to our own set of opinions, we are not
Entitled to our own set of facts.

It is accurate that the quest for the "truth" is filled with obstacles
And sometimes changes with objective investigation,
But the journey must not be filled with hate and intimidation.

We have long ago agreed that the ultimate process for resolving
Our disputes rests with our judiciary.
That is why the politization of some of our courts of law
At both the state and federal level
Appear to have lost sight of the importance of objectivity
And the special role they play in the preservation of our Democracy.

The rule of law upon which our Republic is grounded
Relies on this fundamental value in the search for truth.

Our judicial system held against the forces of misinformation and
corruption
And the planned conspiracy by some for an insurrection
After our last election.

The question that keeps me up at night
Is whether we have the collective will
To "handle the truth" – Only time will tell.

# The Old Elm Tree

The two boys sat once again under the massive old elm tree
Discussing, and often debating, what they believed to be the most
Important issues impacting their lives – wondering how they could
Persuade their friends to "see".

It mattered not that they were mere adolescents, boys of thirteen
Years of age, teetering between childhood dreams
And early teenage malaise.

They thought of themselves as contemporary knights of the roundtable
Called to a world council of diplomats
Tasked with the responsibility of resolving the threats
Of world destruction unleashed by the potential of nuclear annihilation.

They were the prodigy of life on the planet
When schools instituted "safety protocols"
Which required children to drop to the classroom floor
And scramble under their desks
In an effort to "protect" them from the horror of nuclear war.

It was a time when some in their community constructed bomb shelters
Dug deep within their backyards.
When on every street corner in the country's metropolitan locations
And even in small rural towns
Yellow signs were erected indicating
The nearest location of government bomb shelters
And of unspoken fear.
At a time of stiff upper-lip
No tears.

So, the boys dreamed of a plan which would resolve international conflict
Through governmental reconciliation.
Of course, this subject and others they discussed
Were uninteresting to most thirteen-year-old kids, for sure.
But they were undeterred. They were determined to have a future.

Some decades have passed
And the old elm is gone.
Raised by wind and storm.
Many of the boys' dreams
Have also been ripped and torn.

One has become a wine connoisseur
The other a humble soothsayer.

Yet, on days filled with reports of school shootings,
Pandemic deaths, and divisive displays of ignorance,
I think of these boys who dreamed of better days
Achieved by love and reconciliation.

May their advice be remembered by the Nation.

# The Call

I received a call the other day
From a friend who lives far away.

He was concerned about the state of our planet
And said he felt helpless and without hope.
I understood that he was asking me
To throw him a rope of sorts
To pull him from a depression
Which had engulfed him
And millions of Earth's citizens
As we confront the challenges
Of the Twenty-first Century.

I was humbled that he asked me.

I was quick to respond
And said that we must become sisters and brothers
If we have a chance at all to save this tiny blue marble
From the impact of homo sapiens
After the Fall.

We have never learned that our existence is fragile
And our time is finite.
Certainly not guaranteed at all.

Since we have emerged from the cave,
We have found innumerable ways to create walls.
To divide ourselves from each other
To claim superiority over one another.

The color of our skin, the choice of one's religion,
Or to not believe at all
Has been used by those who profit from stoking fear of the "others"
Instead of celebrating the wonder and beauty of our diversity
And yet, not lose track of our similarities.
What each of us brings to the Clan of homo sapiens.

Well, he asked, "What can we do to secure the planet from
Armageddon?
I answered that we must listen.
To the messages written on the cavern wall
By those who have come before.
About the horrors of war and the paths we can take
To insure for those who come after,
A world with less hate.

But before I could complete my thought,
My friend said that he had a knock on his door.
After a moment or two he returned to the phone
To say that his pizza had arrived and that my thoughts
On saving the human race would have to wait for another day.

Much to my exasperation, he concluded that "Nothing matters, life is
Too short. May just as well enjoy the cheese, pepperoni, and onion
Pizza pie. We are all going to die." I wished him well and ended our call.
What did I expect after all?

# Staring Down the Bully

Standing at the precipice
Staring over the edge into the abyss
Images of death and destruction
Resonate with all who have taken the pledge
To stand together, to participate in a show of force
Against those who would intimidate the "others"
Into submission with military force and occupation.

Capitulation in the short term may avoid
Immediate confrontation.
But we have learned since we have emerged from the cave
That, sadly, force must be met with force
If the bully is to be constrained
From possessing absolute power.

The choice is ours.

# Resolve and Resist — Slava Ukraini

Another day has passed.
The sand in the hourglass has silently shifted to the bottom
One wonders what is left to be said
Whether anything written will be read.

Will time be the Victor?
Or will the message outlast the inevitable conclusions of the task?

They stand like lonely travelers who reach the edge of a cavern ledge
Shouting to the other side warning of the dangers coming from behind
Only to hear echoes of their screams
Tumbling like helpless pebbles in a turbulent stream.

Images of crying children placed in the crosshairs of ignorance and hate
fill their minds.
Dropping to their knees, they sob for the innocent and the kind
Who will be left behind.

Oh, the impotence of the Poet's words and prose shake him to his core.
What more can be done? Is the only path war?
They must be stopped, he thought.

He rose to his feet with a resolve he had not felt before.
A mist the death and destruction which may lie ahead — it must be said
No military machine can ever destroy the cry for freedom and liberty
No, the bully cannot hide. He cannot cremate the truth.

The "victors" can always write their version of history.
But somewhere packed in vessels hidden deep within the cave
Will be written the truth.
The actual truth of the terror perpetrated — the genocide created.
There must be an accounting. The journey must continue. It cannot end.

There are messages to be written in hope that they will someday be read.
The cries of the children must be heard screaming from the cave.
"Stand up to the Bear. Be unafraid. The future of the free world is in
your hands.
Be brave. Capitulation is not an option. We will be watching."

# Don't Look Away

Look away they say
Its not your fight.
Look away from the naked aggression
Upon a peaceful sovereign nation.
Look away from the propaganda
Which attempts to destroy hundreds of years
Of a proud people.
Look away from the limp lifeless body of the child
In its father's arms.
Look away from the flesh splashed
Across the apartment walls of civilians
Too old to escape the bombs.
Look away they are the "others"
They have strange names.
Their language is not ours – we can send flowers.
Look away it is too late.

But we know in the depth of our souls
That John Donne's warning was right.

"No man is an island entire of itself;
Every man is a piece of the continent
A part of the main…Any man's death diminishes me
Because I am involved in Mankind…Therefore, never
Send to know for whom the Bell tolls: it tolls for thee."
WE MUST NOT LOOK AWAY.

# A Dream on the Train to Safety

As days collapse into nights
And the sounds of the train wheels
Clack rhythmically against the old rusty tracks
She holds her baby close to her breast
Hoping that the beating of her heart
Will calm her child's fear and dry her tears,
If only for a little while.

She is but one of millions of refugees
Fleeing the death and destruction of an unprovoked
Attack on her nation.
The train is packed with women and children
Trying to escape the bombing of civilians.
All wondering if they will ever see again
Their families left behind
Or their beloved Ukraine.

In an attempt to steady herself and regain
Some sense of self-control,
The woman closes her eyes and tries to remember
A joyous time which can sustain her,
At least, momentarily, from succumbing
To the chaos surrounding her.

She thinks of a happier time
When she prepared meals for family and friends
At her home in Kyiv. And, the kind "thank you" she always received.
One occasion came to mind. It was a family tradition.
One which celebrated the coming of Spring – the Easter Meal.

Surprisingly, she thought not of the food or drink
Which was always in great supply.
Instead she was reminded of the exchange of pysanky
Amongst her guests.

These delicately designed eggs, while beautiful to behold,
Were a special symbol of resurrection.
Representations of the creation of life
Coming from darkness into light.

She prayed that the pysanka
She had carefully packed and placed in her only bag
Would once again return home unbroken
When the destruction of her country ceases.
When out of the ashes Ukraine
Will also be resurrected.
That peace through strength will come again.

# A Conversation

The old man said, "Come sit down beside me, Son.
Let us discuss both the living and the dead.
Much has been said about the sadness
That surrounds us now. Most of it is true.
But there is so much more that should come through.

While images of crying children and destruction of a nation
Fill our thoughts and invade our dreams,
To continue we must give our lives meaning by
Planning for reconstruction.
We must dream of a world rising from the ashes
Produced by the actions of war criminals,
And find strength from those who out of love
For freedom and liberty, will help us protect our
Fledgling democracy. We must join with
The "others" who have risen in our defense
Who also share our fundamental values
Those which connect the Children of Light and
which separate men from beasts.

Please don't misunderstand what I am saying.
We should not dismiss the destruction;
The unconscionable murder of innocent
Men, women, and children lying in the streets.
There must be an accounting. Their deaths demand that.
But their lost should have meaning beyond retribution.
Their unjustified slaughter must also give birth
To a nation and a world which sends a powerful message
To those who come after.
That no petty dictator who would endanger the world
With threats of nuclear war will ever succeed.

That regardless of our multitude of cultures and different creeds,
There is one value which unites us all.
It is a call which has been heard from across the millennia
From our Kinsmen of the cave – Freedom, Son, freedom."

# And This Too Shall Pass

From darkness into light
A journey which does not come
Without a fight.
Sabers rattle and it is easy to be overcome
By hate a mist our tears
And succumb to our deepest fears.

It has been said that, "an eye for an eye blinds the whole world."
It is an important insight as the Children of Light
Begin to unite
In an effort to preserve their liberty.

But it must also be said that the annihilation of a nation
Must be met with overwhelming force.
While this action must include counter attacks,
It also must demonstrate a willingness to show compassion
For all who reject war and the potential use of Satan's Clubs.

In the end – after hostilities cease,
The seeds of peace must be sown
By those who remember that today's
Vanquished enemy must become
Willing partners in the future survival of humanity.

# The Little Song Bird - (Amellia Anisovych)

She is seven years of age.
When she stands on stage
She sings with the innocence
And love that only a child can project.
She sings her national anthem
To thousands of citizens standing in the
Cold and darken night.
Each holds a candle to signal their support
For her and her country now under attack.
She also sings to the world – to all freedom loving people –
Listening from across the planet.
She symbolizes the strength and hope of her besieged country.

For a moment in time her voice fills the air with the sweetness
That only a child's voice can create – it reflects an innocence and love
That unites all freedom loving citizens of the world
Who are rising up to protect all those who come in peace,
But are willing to stare down the Bear who threatens those who
Seek liberty.

Let her nation's anthem remind us all
Of what has been written on the cavern wall
That, sadly, force is sometimes necessary
For freedom to be preserved.
Liberty cannot be bought – it must be won.
May the candles flickering in the dark tonight, produce the light
Which will spur the free world to unite
To protect her nation from further destruction
And be steadfast in their support for its reconstruction.

Sing, little song bird, sing.

# On A Clear Day

To fly amongst the Maples,
To soar above the trees.
To catch the Wind's current, so easily.

Let my spirit transcend,
Let it ride on a cloud
Drifting over the Heartland
Across the prairie's rich sod
To the factories of the Great Lakes
And the Eastern hub.

Where is it written that
We have the right to endanger this
With the use of Satan's Clubs?

All that has been written
And that we shall ever write
Can never justify another demonstration
Of nuclear might.

Naïve, foolish, some self-anointed experts say.
"To be secure you must be strong. There is no other way."

I agree that strength is the key, but I humbly submit
That strength can be gleaned also through careful compromise
And understanding – not by the construction of additional
Missile pits.
Examine the meaning of strength
By observing two trees
Against a fierce wind.

Is it the mighty oak with thick trunk and limb,
Or, the nimble willow resilient and trim
Which withstands the force of the hurricane wind?

There are no secrets in what I say.
But I do feel compelled as I pass this way
To remind you to watch the willow
Sway against the gale force
And to warn you to stand clear from the oak
As it is ripped from its source.

Opening the Door

Messages Lost and Found

# The Messenger

He came in a dream
A mist the terror and screams.
Clad in a white gown
Glowing against the darkness surrounding him.

He held a tablet with undecipherable script
Emblazoned on it.
He glided toward the man
In an effort to help him see.

The warmth of his presence
Surrounded the man
With an indescribable sense of love and empathy
As if to tell him that nothing could harm him
And to be unafraid.

Others could be seen gathered behind him
Standing on what appeared to be a balcony
Beckoning him to join them.

But then an unspoken message was sent,
"Open your mind."
The script on the tablet could be read.
"Now is not your time. Be assured we will welcome you.

But there remains much to be done before you come."

Suddenly, the man awoke. Trying not to shake.
Was this a spiritual encounter or a mistaken interpretation?
Whatever the source of this moment in time,
The sense of love and oneness experienced then
Sustains him as he tries to
Open the door
So that others can "see"
The paths that can be taken
To appreciate the beauty
that surrounds us all
to be unafraid as we are challenged by obstacles
which must be overcome
In our individual journeys for freedom.

# Last Night

Last night in my dream I was a "seer"
Transformed before my eyes was our planet so clear.

Wealth, poverty, love and hate,
God's creatures incarnate.

Ignorance and insight competing for control.
Testing the courage of those few Souls;
Earth's citizens, black, red, yellow, brown, and white.
Those who have inherited the inner light.

The knowledge that peace shall only be achieved
By listening to the timeless rhythms,
So long ago given, given – last night in my dream.

# Coming Thru to the Other Side

Walk through the void with old
And beautiful souls.
Challenged by jealousy, bias, and self-interest
It takes its toll.

Yet, raised to confront with courage and grace.
Trying to find our place.
How to withstand the demands of now
In search for Tao?

Fly with the winds;
Dig deep within;
It has been given.

# Questioning the Process

The packaging of one's thoughts
For public consumption.
What a presumption.

Put the blocks together in neat rows.
Maybe they will soothe some souls.

But where will it take us?
What words will solve the endless complexities?

The journey must continue
If for no other reason
Then the process confronts our fear
Of the unknown.

# Trying to Find Balance

I sometimes wonder what it would be like
To live in a world
Of Good without Evil.
Occupied only by the Children of Light
A "peaceful kingdom" if you like.
One which refuses to tolerate hate
A place of recycled souls finding eternal grace.

But, much to my despair, I am, sadly, aware
That we have yet to achieve this aspirational
Goal of human perfection.
Upon reflection, I am reminded of observations
Recorded some twenty-five hundred years ago.
One in particular seems to steady me and always
Brings some balance to my quest to maintain my sanity
In this cycle of "reality".

It is an observation from the Tao Te Ching
Written by Lao Tzu, it is said.
It is one of eighty visions of the universe
and our interactions within it.
It provides recommendations as to what course
We should choose as we cycle through
our time on the Earth plane.

Lao Tzu wrote, "Under heaven all can see beauty
As beauty only because there is ugliness.
All can know Good because there is evil…"
At the core of Taoist thought is the belief in what has been described
As the "unity of opposites."

Recognition of this "truth" allows us to understand
The essence of all things – black/white, life/death
Ignorance/enlightenment, happiness/sadness, etc.

Acceptance of this duality in all things does bring a sense
Of balance in this mystical process we call life.
It helps to remind us of the inter-connectedness of our universe
And its functioning.
But for those immersed in Western thought
Who have been taught the "truths" discovered via the scientific method
And the all consuming need to control the universe,
Its is agonizingly difficult to accept the inseparability
Of good and evil.

It may be that the best that we can do is to maximize
The good and minimize the evil
And continue to dream.

# A Tribute to Thich Nhat Hanh

Life is not a zero-sum game.
It is filled with experiences which are sad and joyful.
We are left with an amalgam
Of what remains
What is important is that we appreciate the process
And remember that in the end
There are no winners or losers
Only souls who have been permitted to play in the game.

So let us all refrain, for a moment, from the all too human response
To some momentary victory or loss
And give thanks to those who reminded us of the cost
Of claiming superiority over one or another.
Instead of celebrating our commonality as sisters and brothers.

# Free Will: A Suggestion

We come in alone.
And we go out alone.
In the mean time we have a choice to make.

Find more love than hate
Or make the worst mistake.
Chose love, do not partake in the dark path of hate.

The decision is ours to make.

# The Challenge

Yellow post-it notes and paper clips
Strewn across the desk.
Tools to help keep emotions and thoughts in check.

The process of recording messages from within
Constantly given
From experiences past and present
Demanding to be given birth in hope
That they will be heard on the planet Earth.

"Seek and you shall be given"
The messages create a rhythm.
Listen.
The communications are clear for those who ask
The question:" Where do we go from here?"

The answer has been given from time immemorial –
from the "seers" who came before.
All of whom have provided paths to open the door.

Quiet your mind. Listen for the sound of one hand clapping.
Understand that love not hate will ameliorate the fear
Of hopelessness which sometimes appears from the chaos
Created by ignorance and greed.

It is our obligation to listen and be determined
That the forces of darkness shall not succeed.

# Thinking Aloud

Ludwig Wittgenstein once wrote about the Limits of Language
And its impact upon our capability of understanding each other.

His philosophical observations which have triggered debate
Amongst scholars for over one hundred years have produced
A multitude of conclusions
which can bring one to tears.

With no intent to belittle his important observation,
It must be said that language is but one form of communication.
Our utterances and dreams, whether written and presented
Via papyrus, the printing press, or from images painted on a cavern wall,
Are all, in their own, messages sent from our souls.

The written word can be beautiful in its purest form.
It can trigger emotion from the deepest and most intimate
Experiences of our lives.
But it also can be used as an evil instrument in an attempt
To marginalize that which is non-conforming or different.

Of course, our realities are shaped not only by what is written
But also by what is smelled, heard, or touched.
Our senses, some would suggest, are not limited to these techniques
Of "seeing"

Instead for centuries some have insisted that separate realities
Exists which can be experienced by tapping into the Karmic Book.
Others are convinced that a multitude of parallel universes exist
Competing for recognition by those of us willing
To explore and listen.

I cannot validate the experiences of others, as Wittgenstein has proposed,
But I can urge all who are confused and yearn for "answers"
To actually – Stop and smell a rose.

The result will be different for each of us.
One person may describe the fragrance verbally,
While another may write of its physical beauty.
And yet another may communicate with a simple smile.

It may be that the written or spoken word
May have its limits – but –
Coupled with our senses, it can be
But one more instrument, if we choose to "see"
The majesty of our lives
As we cycle through to eternity.

# Question Asked and Answered

What obligation do we have to one another?
Some would answer none at all.
Life is a zero-sum game.
Those with the most toys in the end
Win after all.

Just look around, they say. Look at the definition of success
We have all been programed to believe.
Success equates to grabbing the most money
Through any means from a society built
On corruption and greed.

Its man against man. Survival of the fittest.
If you do not understand this, you really are naïve.

When I read or hear this I am not surprised
But I remained amazed.
What life experiences have they encountered
That would create such callousness, such an absolute disregard
For others? How were they raised?

Did they not get chosen on the play ground for some childhood game?
Or, were they unsuccessful in finding a date for the high school prom?
Were they targeted by the "mean girls" and constantly rebuffed when at
The lunch room table?

Of course, there are many more truly damaging experiences
Which should not be made to appear frivolous. Unlike those already
noted.
For example, an abusive home life, the effect of homelessness,
Or the impact of being unsuccessful in overcoming poverty's strife.

There is no intention here to provide a moralistic response to the
question posed.
Much has already been proposed by both sectarian and secular "seers"
both past and present.
Some have offered guidance by offering moral codes by which to live,
While others have suggested transcendental methods to gain
Spiritual insight about our oneness with each other.

All of these prophets who have come before
And some who walk among us
Remind us, in differing ways,
What even the most cynical eventually learn.

That which is tangible may be temporarily useful and may
Bring momentary joy – but is often discarded.
That which is eternal lies deep within us and is never forgotten.
Because it evolves from the heart.

# Celebrate the Intangible

Much can be learned as the wheel turns
And life provides us with glimpses of true understanding.
It was once written that while that which is tangible in our lives
Provides us structure, order and sometimes profit,
That which is intangible and ever evolving
Is equally important.

It is true that goals achieved are wondrous things.
Sometimes they are accompanied with trophies.
But too often we forget the people we met and the help we
Received along the way which bound us together.
We became a team, not without hardship and conflict,
But which ultimately produced friendships
Long after the prizes achieved
are placed in the closet and forgotten.

In fact, the love and exhilaration produced by some
Accomplishment with the support of others
Often carry us through the failures inevitable in the process called life.

In a society which too often praises the tangible "accomplishments"
And evaluates success as the sum total of all things acquired,
It would be wise to recognize the importance of the intangible
The true essence of life:

The beautiful stillness of the night;
The sound of rain on an old tin roof;
A call from a long - ago friend;
Loves lost found again;
Recognition that all things past begin again in time;
Acceptance that the script may have
A beginning, middle, and an end.
But an understanding that the play has just begun.
Our roles may change as we travel around the Sun,
But much remains to be done.

# 4 a. m.

Empty vacuums of purposelessness
Infinite ticking of time,
Grasping for "truths",
But none seem to be mine.

# The Unity of Opposites

Every waking moment of being
Seems to concentrate on feeling.
Feelings of love and hate
Of misery and happiness
Of fulfillment and emptiness

Their inseparability continually haunts us.
There seems to be no shelter left.
No mystical refuge for our souls.
Only the constant reminder of the
Endless contradictions.

Yet, the contradictions take us one step beyond
The artificial intricacies of life
To the search for our place in its beautiful simplicity.

# Listening

What a joy it is to feel the excitement renewed
Of the long-lost sensation of solitude.
To hear the mellow quietness of the night
To stop and remind ourselves to not lose sight
Of all the wonders that transpire
Outside of human auspices.

The rising of the sun, the melting of the snow
Even the turbulence of stormy seas.
All are continual reminders of our brief encounter with life.

If only we can continue to open our eyes
With our minds
We will be able to walk the narrow path
Between awareness and darkness.

# Understanding the Danger

The endless need for recognition
Hangs over our lives like an elastic web.
It bends with our constant fluctuation
Of purpose, yet still entraps us
In the "I" of our realities.

Looking for an opening in the seemingly impenetrable
Prison walls
Consciously, and too often, unconsciously,
We sublimate "I" into differing causes for "they".
But the façade only temporarily
Relieves our fear of freedom.

# Modern Man

We build great monuments
To our towering intellect
Yet, we end up destroying ourselves
Instead of the intended "evil" insect.

The Moon is but a mere instant away,
But, our so-called "leaders" stress
That world oneness must wait for another day.
Who in hell are we fooling anyway?

# Centuries Have Passed

Centuries have passed but nothing has changed
The robin still comes as the harbinger of Spring.

Centuries have passed but nothing has changed
Young children still cry for their mother's breast.

Centuries have passed but nothing has changed
Men still dream of the day they will be free.

Centuries have passed but nothing has changed
The deer retreat to the mountain's top first sign of winter.

Centuries have passed but nothing has changed
The hunter cleans his gun and hopes for a snowfall.

Centuries have passed but nothing has changed
Turn the wheel, turn the wheel, turn.

Traveling away and always return
Looking for love but finding hate
Centuries have passed but nothing has changed.

# Reflections Off the Lake

Driving in a circle
Searching for the light.

Remembering the past
Trying to escape the fight.

Mining the recesses of memory
For the moments of love
When hope and future reigned above.

It has been so long since the fulfillment of a Dream

Where to go from here; what path to take?
How to leave a legacy of faith
Yet teach the skills of survival for his sake.

Torn by the Ought and the Is
Can't see the beginning becoming blinded by the end
What message can we send
Other than: the circle never ends.

# Choosing

Sacrifice, solace, sincerity, and sin
Pulling and pushing, searching within.
All to find "answers" for kin.

Drown in the sorrow that loneliness brings
To those who would confront the Kings.

Risk the unthinking security that sameness provides
From glimpsing priceless values thrust aside.
Destroyed by greed, distrust and self,
Constantly subsumed by the quest for wealth.

'Tis wealth the villain or are we simply deceived?
Too focused on now to clearly perceive
The keys of the cycles
To which we are eternally fixed.

Look to the sunset. Surely it is there
A mist our hopes, our dreams, and tears.

A glimmer of love, untainted – pure.
Love greater than country, greater than self
Rooted in our souls screaming to appear.

Be courageous, be open, risk all.
Our lives are simply the conduit to answer the Call.

# Nature's Reprieve
# From Inside Looking Out

# Thank You

The giggle of a child
A beautiful woman preening before a mirror
The fragrance of a rose
A snowflake tickling your nose
A Harvest Moon
The gurgling sound of a country stream
The call of a song-bird "phebee, phebee, phebee"
The power of Sunrise
The melancholy of Sunset
Life's wonders – Let us not forget.

# From My Window

As I open my eyes from the darkness of the night,
I observe, through my frosted bedroom window
All the miraculous events
That the primordial mother has performed as I slept.

She has left on the roofs of all the neighboring houses
A thin layer of her purity.
If you glance quickly, it is almost as if she has placed beautiful
Table clothes of white linen precisely fitting the contours of each roof.

Somehow, she has awakened the sparrows.
They seem to be winging from tree to tree,
Chirping as they fly, that life still exists
Regardless of man's efforts to silence it.

She has also left signs of her overwhelming power.
The barren branches of the surrounding trees
Seem to stand as a symbol of death
Only to be resurrected by the warmth of the morning Sun.

I beg you. Just look through any window.

# Wondering

The air is cold and crisp
And the Earth seems to be preparing
Its old crust for another Winter.

I wonder if Mother Nature has ever heard
Of base-board heating?

# No Regrets

She is alone, and crying now;
Wondering why he has gone.

She remembers that his only treasures
Were not part of the pleasures that she embraced.
He talked of trees and the wind
Almost as if they were his adopted family.

But what did he know of trees and the wind?
He spoke of himself and his life as a private crusade
For something he called oneness.
But what did he know of himself?

# On A Cold Winter's Morn

Ice covers the branches of the trees surrounding the old house.

It glistens in early morning sun
And forms rows of sickles across the rooftop
Constantly expanding
Showing no sign that they will stop.

While logic insists that their expansion
Should be interrupted by a sharp blow
From a broom

There is something that can't resist
Watching each frozen spike's evolution
As but one more of Nature's solution
To the magical interplay between
The Sun and ice
On a cold Winter's day.

# A Mountain Pond

Up a winding road just before you reach the Notch
(a long-ago road blasted out of massive granite rock)
Sits a little pond.

Its creation is a story worth telling.
At least I think it is.
Because like all things worth preserving
It exemplifies the virtues of understated
Expertise, stubbornness, and just dumb luck.

The tale begins with a young couple seeking to build
A post and beam home. It was initially to be used
As a summer refuge from their hectic professional lives
Out of state.

They purchased a ten-acre piece of property
The locals thought it was a big mistake.
The property was situated on a knoll with a rather steep slope.
Only about two acres of buildable land could support
The home's construction.

While much consternation ensued as to whether the dream
Post and beam should be pursued,
A foundation was eventually dug and a beautiful structure was
completed.
The interior displayed a stairway made of cherry wood
And a twenty-eight-foot-tall fireplace
Made with fieldstone from a nearby quarry.
A masterpiece of masonry work created
By a high school chum.

There was, however, the not so small detail to be determined.
Where would the necessary water be extracted to accommodate
The house's functioning?

It was now time to secure the assistance of those with expertise.
So, after much searching, the young homeowners were directed to a
dowser.

He came with a good reputation and was kind enough
To fit them into his busy schedule.

He had the look of a master surgeon
Confident in his training and that he would, indeed,
Have a successful outcome in the search for water.

After a relatively short inspection of the property
With dowser stick in hand,
He reported his finding that water was absolutely present
In the location indicated.
And that he knew an excellent well driller
Who would complete the task.

The driller was hired and the project was to begin
With all deliberate speed. No questions asked.
Simultaneous to the adventure of exploring for water
Was the creation of a leach field and the shaping of the mountain side
For a road to the house and the creation of an earthen mound
Which would be planted with a variety of trees
To create additional privacy.

The excavator was well respected by the locals
Who frequented the country store at the bottom of the mountain.
He had a reputation of honesty. But he was a man of few words.
He also had the smile of a Cheshire cat. Small in stature
But sturdy in build.

He sat atop his tractor like Hannibal
Sitting on his elephant—leading his troops
Across the Alps and into battle.

He watched without comment as the well driller banged his machine
Through layer after layer of rock
Never communicating his suspicion
Of the soil condition of the sloping mountain side.

He liked the young couple as they did him.
But he was there to shape the landscape and build a road
Not to interfere with his opinion.

After numerous telephone calls to the home owners now back at their jobs
Away from the construction site, the well driller provided them
With calls telling them about each day's failure to strike water — it kept
them up at night.
"Down five hundred feet, no water." "Six hundred feet, no luck."
"We are at six hundred and fifty. Do you want to go further?"
(It should be noted that the cost of per foot drilling was way beyond
Estimated projections).
With great reservation, a decision was made – "Go down another
One hundred feet and then stop."
The couple were reminded of the old saying "if you are in for a penny,
You are in for a pound," and they prayed that water would be at last
found.

The driller called back at the end of the day with news that water
Had been found down in the rocky aquifer seven hundred and twenty
feet and

That he was positive that the amount secured would fulfill the
homeowners needs.

A week or two later a twelve-hour trip ensued back to the new
homestead
In an effort to fulfill familial responsibilities, inspect the status of the newly
Drilled well, and to discuss final landscaping decisions.

Upon arrival, sitting atop his massive excavating machine,
Was Jim.

After a brief greeting with him,
I noticed that he wanted to tell me something
That maybe he should have told me before.
He said he had followed the saga of our seven-hundred and twenty-foot
well
With careful observation.
He wondered if we had been notified by the Dowser or the well driller
Of the noticeable soil moisture in the front of the home on its lower
slope?
I said, "Nope." I told him I had been focused on other pressing issues
regarding

The post and beam's construction and other work-related problems in
the Flatlands
To the West.
"Well, he said, I didn't want to interfere, and I guess I should have said
something
Earlier, but I think you have a spring over there in front of the house. If you
Want I can just scoop out a hole and see.
If I am right. In a day or two it should fill up, if there is water. If so, you
May want to consider digging a pond."

He knew he was correct about the existence of
Water. There was enough, it turned out, to fill a
Twelve-foot-deep half-acre pond which still remains
Three decades later.

The local selectwoman eventually approved a permit for the
Construction of the pond after much discussion.

Many of the locals from the small mountain country store
Were in disbelief. One by one they timidly came to the property
For closer inspection. While some were willing to admit that the house
Was beautiful and that the pond added a special quality to the property,
other original naysayers remained silent out of a begrudging respect for
the builder and to not appear as idiots.

It is amazing how some old axioms ring true
"Imitation is the best form of flattery"

Not more than two years after the excavation of the little pond,
Did three more appear on the slopes of the mountain – created by
The soft-spoken Vermonter who was unwilling to interfere.

It, however, never ceases to amaze me, how wonderful it would have been
If Jim had told me sooner of his "suspicion".
My anxiety would have been lowered and my saving account would have
been
Much fuller.

# Coming to an Understanding

It was a warm late Spring morning
And he was determined to step outside
To fulfill his Winter's long yearning.

To once again smell the fragrance of hyacinths
And honeysuckles rapidly emerging around the old
Split-rail fence
And to inspect the garden now free from its blanket of snow and ice.
And to determine if the tulip bulbs planted last Fall
Had survived the cold of winter and the scavenging of miscreant
squirrels
Who always seemed to refuse to play nice and co-operate
With his plan to fill the landscape with color
In a loving salute to a mother who had long passed.

But, he thought, even if the tulips didn't survive, the plan
Would not be totally lost.
The daffodils would soon fill in any barren spots
As would a few well-placed pots.

So after a brief inspection of the emerging garden,
He decided to finish his cup of tea
In relative tranquility.

Sitting in his secluded spot dreaming of the English Cottage-garden
He would create, he began to meditate.

But his brief daydream was suddenly interrupted
By the sound of crows crackling
Announcing the presence of an uninvited visitor.

Down the long path below his bench
Was a small but distinguished looking fox.

He had observed the fox on a few occasions from his kitchen window
Often trotting thru the woodlot
High on a knoll following along a well-traveled deer run.

He always appeared to be on an important mission
Unwilling to stop and have a conversation.
But this time he seemed to have a different calculation.

To reach the path he had traveled many times before
Would require more time and certainly more effort.
So, the fox thought, a new plan was needed which would cut his travel
Time to his destination.

After much thought he came to the conclusion
That he needed the human sitting at the top of the path
To give his permission.
This would require a conversation.

Before he uttered a word, he gently took a step forward
Up the incline.
But he was met with a bellowing sound of rejection.

The man yelled, "Don't be so lazy. Take the path you have always
followed.
I have but one sanctuary. You have many. I don't mean to be unfriendly
But while your journey may be a bit longer traveling the old run, you
Will be free from other creatures like me
Who may not appreciate your right to be free.
Good luck in your travels. Enjoy your day. As I will mine."

The fox, at first, was sadden that his plan of a short-cut
Was not approved. But, he thought, the human was not
Being rude. He was actually stating the truth.

We all have difficult paths to take. Sometimes the shortest
Is simply not the best — for goodness sake.
He then turned to his normal path
But stopped one more time to register his appreciation
For the conversation without confrontation
And wished the human well.

# A Breach of Contract

The chipmunks and the gardener had come to an agreement
At least that is what the man had thought.
The chipmunks could house themselves in his stonewall
And forage on the yearly supply of nuts fallen from
The trees on the property.

The gardener had even accepted the fact that
They would occasionally burrow into his well-maintained yard
For all kinds of tasty morsels.

But the compact with these unappreciative tenants was breached
When they set their sights on the tender leaves of the Japanese Maples
And other perennials just coming to Spring bloom.

There was no room for debate
As to the terms of the contract.
No reasonable interpretation that such activity
Was reflective of the gardener's intention.

The relevant clause in their covenant states,
Without equivocation, that such behavior renders
The agreement null and void.

It was clearly signified that such breach of the contract
Would trigger penalties providing the injured party with
Damages for lost plants and for pain and suffering
Created by the breaching party. But how to enforce the contract?

A precedent must be established that such behavior will be met
With serious consequences.

But then reality set in – "Come to your senses silly gardener.
Did you really believe that you could establish
The rule of law where good-faith does not exist between the parties?"

It appears, the gardener thought, the only solution was to hope
That Harry the Hawk would come again to the garden
And permanently solve the problem.

# A New Addition to the Garden

It has been a year or so
But not that long
Since the young lilac bush was planted lovingly in the ground.

It was found a mist other shrubs of the same variety
But this new acquaintance called out to him.

Unlike the others placed carefully in neat rows
With some stacked on wooden bins
Its branches were sturdy and it appeared to be a relatively
New addition to the nursery.

Its purchase was swift
Made without a blink of an eye.
Off to the garden it traveled
To be separated from its pot and carefully
Planted by hand and shovel.
It was to join the other shrubs and flowers
Already beginning their yearly evolution.

The garden's residents welcomed their adopted friend
With silent applause and a sigh of relief.
That the empty barren spot in their community would be
Filled with beautiful purple buds and a fragrance to be enjoyed
By all.

But it has taken surprisingly longer than expected
Since the young plant's inauguration that new
Buds have appeared.

There were no signs of disease
Or branches chomped off by foraging deer.
There became an unspoken fear.

This will be the year, they thought,
That would tell the tale
Of success or failure of the purchase and the impact
Of Winter's onslaught.

By mid-Spring the fear and loathing
Of the young lilac's neighbors
Was finally set aside.

The little lilac bush began to display
The beautiful buds and wonderful fragrance
They had all wished for
The season before.

It was now secure. And with a little help from its friend,
It would reach maturity.
Taking its rightful place within the community.

Maurie Harrington —

# Fly Fishing on the Battenkill

I was once told that life would begin again
If only I just went fly fishing.

So I dutifully marched off to purchase
Some essential gear in an effort
To guarantee success in my new endeavor.

I was promised that with a little patience and practice
Of flipping my wrist,
The pole and line would automatically land
My fly where a hungry fish could not resist.

Off I went down dusty backroads and through meadows
Filled with bramble bush and yarrow,
To an embankment beside my beloved river.
Convinced that a beautiful rainbow trout
Would be mine in no time and would soon be my dinner.
But, for at least an hour, and cast after cast,
My line became tree limb and prickly bush entangled.

Undeterred I climbed down the embankment and into the stream
Searching for a spot to cast my line
Where fish and fly would combine.
Yet, after what seemed to be an eternity,
It became clear that my dream of becoming
The angler king, would have to wait until next year.

Nevertheless, I knew that the real purpose of my adventure
Had been fulfilled.
My mind was quiet and my spirit was still.
Oh, how I love the Battenkill.

# The Upper Hollow Road

It seems like only yesterday
But a century has passed.

The road still remains unpaved providing passage
Over dirt and gravel hard pressed.

Winter's ice and snow still melt and create ruts
Which must be constantly filled by village road crews
Who pray for the end of mud season.
And for good reason.

Why they ask shouldn't the road be paved
And end this yearly struggle? It is a reasonable request.
But it always creates a kerfuffle.

Beside the predictable concern by taxpayers
Of the cost of such a venture,
There exists an unspoken reason which serves
As a yearly rejection of such a suggestion.

It is a collective understanding that the road
Is more than a passage to the multimillion dollar
Vacation homes of city dwellers who occupy
The Hollow.

Instead the road is a symbol of times past.
Of old teams of horses pulling their loads of milk
Down to the little cheese factory at the bottom of the hill.
Of children trekking up and down its dusty path
To and from school.

Indeed, one has to conjecture that refusal to pave the road
Is a stubborn notion to not lose track of what once was
And of the fear that it may never come back.

# An Ode to Vermont

As I write from self-imposed exile,
Created by economic concerns,
I often think of her almost unbelievable beauty,
My familial roots, and how I can return.

How does one express the joy I feel, as I travel up the steep mountain
Road where once my grandmother asked grandfather if their
Old car "had another gear" – I can only surmise that he gave
Her a reassuring response, "Nothing to fear, nothing to fear, my Dear."

Or, the happiness which engulfs me when I am surrounded by birch
trees
Standing as sentinels strategically planted centuries ago,
In an effort to protect the little village from wind and snow.

As I travel pass, house after house, each painted white with green
shutters,
I am filled with pride for my ancestorial brothers
Who answered the call to join other men in a town called Bennington.
To stand and be counted in an effort to preserve their freedom
And to declare their independence.

They were a different breed of citizens.
They would fight and die for individual liberty but also,
For the importance of community – the collective interest of all citizens
was essential.
They understood that the roots of liberty were attached to the protection
Of one another.

The struggles of survival in the wilderness taught them
And their forefathers, that liberty could only be achieved by
Collective commitment to certain values.
They believed as John Locke had once written before,
That each citizen is entitled to the "fruits of (their) labor," as long as
He or she doesn't take more than is needed, and in so doing, deprive

That right to another.

They actually believed in the creed that all men are created equal,
Or at least, should be.
Later generations of families gave their sons, to the cause
Of Abolition and to expand the meaning of Democracy.

The independence reflected in the actions of these small farmers
And shopkeepers still resounds in its citizens.
They remain devoted to personal freedom, yet are equally committed
To the Public Welfare.

The inseparability of these two values enshrined in our Constitution's
Preamble, seem to be built into the character of its citizenry.
Nurtured by its history.

You see, this relatively small strip of land mass carved out by
Hard scrabbled frontier men and women
Is a special place to me. One which through hard work and
Sacrifice gave opportunity to family.

Vermont is more than a location on a map -squeezed between
The White Mountains on its eastern border and the
Adirondacks on the West.
It is also a place in time filled
With memories of children swinging from ropes
Off an old coverage bridge.
Of dusty backroads leading past small farms
And open meadows filled with wildflowers
Just waiting to be noticed before it is time for them
To be mowed.
Of Town Meetings where citizens congregate
To tell their elected "selectmen or women" of their
Opinions and debate.

It is the place where Rockwell painted in illustration
The importance of freedom of speech
And the ugliness of racial discrimination and hate.

These memories, and many more, have sustained me
Over the years.

There is, however, one remembrance which I shall never forget.
One which provides me with some level of comfort, I guess.

It involves a conversation that I once initiated
As I searched for employment that would bring me
Back to my ancestorial roots.

She was a woman of advanced maturity whose family
Had farmed the State's rocky soil for generations.
I told her of my plan to maybe just move back
Absent a guaranteed job – and of my frustration.
She looked at me straight in the eyes, and with honesty
And sincerity reminiscent to past conversations
we had in the days of my youth.
She said, "Son, you can't eat the mountains. Think it through."

A few decades have past and I followed her advice.
Eventually securing employment in the Flatlands to the West –
Begrudgingly becoming an exile, but dreaming of my return.

Yet, I have always wished that I had asked her
What kept her there
Where my soul soars.

My guess is that she would have said to me –
"The history of our family and the community, but there
Is something else that I adore – the mountains, son, my Green
Mountains – even more."

# Fall in the Woodlot

The floor of the forest is covered with a carpet of fallen leaves.
They have created a mosaic pattern of red, gold, and green – a proud display
Reflecting the year's handiwork of photo-synthesis, some say.

Most of the sugar maples are quickly shedding their oft-spring
providing even more brilliance to the beautiful canvas below
On this brisk Autumn day.

The old oak, always the last to succumb to the cold nudges
From the first frost, begrudgingly offers its golden leaves
To the masterpiece being create
For all who pass by and those who stay.

And, not to be overlooked in this divine process of creation
Are the scarlet red leaves of the Japanese Maples and Burning Bushes
Which sparkle in the sunlight of Nature's mystical play.

The now barren clump White Birches
Stand as the steadfast guardians of the woodlot.
Season after season, they reach for the Heavens
Seeking permission to continue their journey.
Or whether they must stop.

Their long white branches appear to be fully formed fingers
Bursting through the canopy of the surrounding trees
Anxiously grabbing the sky above in an effort to secure the woodlot for
another season. Winter is coming.

# A Vermont Walk

The wind is tugging at his neck
Gently prodding him. Warning that time has come
For another cycle in the endless process of life.
Winter will soon arrive.

The leaves have placed a soft warm blanket
On the mountain floor. As if to say, "We know our part
In the eternal scheme. No matter how insignificant it may seem."

Yes, everything appears to be in order. Even the deer sense that
The time has come for them to trek further up the mountain
To avoid the creepy insanity that hunts them down.
Their decision is made. They shall face the danger of starvation
Willingly, to remain free.

Alone, feeling guilty, making his way down the mountain, he feels
An instinctive compulsion to remain
Where life seems to make sense.

But the wind again reminds him that he is not
Yet ready to join them.

He will be back.

# Seasons

Some people seem forlorn
The shedding of Nature's cloak
On an early Autumn's morn.

But sad I will never be.
It is but another reason
For happiness to me.

Because, Nature, in her subtle way,
Is indicating that once again
A year has past
And that our deepest sorrows
Will not last.

Therefore, be not sad when the last leaf
Has fallen to the ground.
There will be another day
Bursting with life and love
That will not know a frown.

# A Celebration

With the coming of Spring
My spirit soars.
The delicate arrival of each new bud evolves into
An explosion of life.
Bursts of Yellow and Green
Of long forgotten fragrances
Resurrects my soul
Another cycle begins.

# Sweet Expectations

Icy Spring rain brings thoughts
Of daffodils struggle for birth.

Messages of life
Exploding from Earth.

Flames from the hearth
Sing a last refrain.

Rejoicing in their importance
But aware of the game.

Hopes and dreams parade through our minds.
Lost friends remembered somewhere in time.

Tears of failure temper our schemes
But undaunted are those who remember the theme:
Believe in thy self
Because embedded within
Lies the spark of the Creator
Lovingly given.

# Memories

# The Past, Present,
and Future Converge

# Memories

Like silent arrows shot by some invisible archer
Meant to awaken our souls of the
Plays once performed
Memories spark our deepest passions
Of love lost; failures endured; successes once achieved;
And of the actions of nations scorned.

They act as important reminders that
Our existence here is part of some grander scheme.
A moment in time. Attempts to be redeemed.

They are snapshots of our actions
Which are to be added to those who have come before.
And those who follow us.

They remind us that our lives and actions
Have meaning – even as we return to dust.

# A moment in Time

Grasping but not holding
Flying without destination
Drifting like a pebble in a turbulent stream.
Floating so effortlessly
Trying to "see"

Where will it end?
Who will I be?
Every memory is a blessing
Until I reach thee.

# A Christmas Gift

It was a cold December night.
You know, the kind that bites both your ears
And nose alike.

Wrapped in coat and scarf with boot buckles
Clicked tight
The boy began his yearly pilgrimage in search
For her special Christmas gift.
It would be unlike any other
placed under the tree, he thought,
"Because it would be from me."

As he walked through the freshly fallen snow
He challenged himself to try to avoid the snowflakes
Tumbling under the street lamps
Before they collected below.

It was a silly game. But no one would know
Except some nosy cat peeking out from a passing window.

But the village Christmas lights were in sight now.
All the store fronts were dressed in garland
And the whole street was aglow.

His trek was almost done.
There in the drugstore window he spotted the prize.
Thank goodness it was not gone.

No matter its small size, it always brought tears to her eyes
When it was unwrapped on Christmas morn.

It was a beautiful blue bottle with distinctive lettering
- Evening in Paris –
A special perfume, the boy thought.
Its fragrance would whisk her away from the troubles of her day
To a place where she could just play.

But what the little boy did not understand
Until he became a man
Was that a mother's love on Christmas day
Comes not from perfume fragrances or beautifully
Wrapped presents from the store.

Instead it comes from the joy on her little boy's face
When he reaches for the gift amongst the Christmas wrapping
Strewn on the floor
And proudly shouts, "Just one more! Merry Christmas, Mom!!"

# Alone

Endlessly, I wonder where you are.
I search for you in the leaves.
I cry for you in the night.
I hear you on the beach.
Yet, always you are beyond my reach.

# A love Lost

What is it I want to say?
I know now may not be the time
But the moment must not pass away.

To love and lost and then to rediscover
Can be something of great happiness
For lovers.

But to have had and then lost
Can there be a greater holocaust?

Maybe now is not our time
But through haste with self in mind
We will never know what life could be
With me with you and you with me.

Emotions cannot erase the freckles on your face
Which I secretly admired when you would retire
Your head tucked in close upon my shoulder
It seemed our love would never be over.

As the Fall leaves turn to brown
On my face there will be a frown.
It will be an expression of love
Not of hate.
One which shall never abate.
For if I have lost my golden reign, and you shall never come again.
I will have truly lost part of me.
Was it really destiny?
Search, search if you must
For in your conscience you must trust.

But remember when the artificial lights of night
Yield helplessly to his touch,
That the moistness which is on your lips
Came from one who is secretly yearning
That it was he who would say, "Good Morning."

# Sunrise

Shuffle through the endless abyss called yesterday
And effortlessly thoughts of abandoned loves reappear.

What once was continues somewhere in the depths
Of our inner-self.
And, like a volcanic eruption inside our heads,
The memories continue to demand recognition.

But the sensation of newly found love
Has reappeared.

Eventually, sad remembrances are swept
Away with thoughts of tomorrow
Helping to illuminate the importance of now.

# A Frequent Visitor

She comes without question.
Prepared to share the warmth
That only her breasts contain.

And knowing that she will not remain,
We touch, become one and then lie still.

Are we insane?
"Yes," she softly responds.
"But insanity is reality
And we are but part of the game."

# Augustus and Gratitude

I have this cat who sits on my lap
And I always wonder why?
Could it be that he sees in me
The love that he has created?

Or, is it simply that he needs a helping hand
To rid himself of those persistent fleas?

Oh, well, whatever the reason
I seem to be pleasing him,
So why should I ask for more?

Maybe it is because that after my faithful rubs,
He always jumps back down on the floor.

# Feeling

Soft warm winds of love
Have captured our minds,
Taking us and leaving them behind.

You move and trembling I respond.
If only I could take you beyond the past and the future
Into the wonder of now.

Long latent emotions of our beings
Are smoldering as never before.

Your eyes shoot forth mysterious
Images of untold tales and my mind soars.

Ladies with long white gowns dance across the universe
And I struggle to know more.

Lovely Lady, lovely lady, stay with me.
Help me see. Help me be free.

# The Old School House

There sits in terrible disrepair
An old structure now abandoned
Covered with an undergrowth of unattended
Honeysuckles and bramble bushes.

No one seems to care that it once stood
Proudly as a one room school house –
A sanctuary of sorts for children of various ages.

They came from across hill and dale
From a landscape dotted with small farms
All struggling to survive.

The children came to dream of faraway places
And to learn to read, write, and to master the
Fundamentals of calculation.
And, for short periods throughout the day,
The school house master/madame would
Permit them to play.

This was a novel event for some of the children
Whose labor was constantly required.
There were cows to be milked
And hay to be brought back to the barn
Before they could retire,
Or even think of having fun.

Therefore, recess at the school yard was joyously received
By all in attendance.
It was a brief reprieve from the everyday hardships
Of rural life in the early Twentieth Century.

So it was for one little girl who walked for a few miles
Over the gentle slopes of the hills surrounding her
Ramshackle house which she shared with her six
Older siblings.

Her early morning journey required her to navigate
Landscapes dotted with juniper trees and a swamp
Created by water flowing to the surface from numerous
Underground springs.

Once she reached the last hill to climb,
She could hear the sound of the school house bell chiming.
Just a few more steps and the day would begin.

While today the number six which is chiseled on the front
Of the building still survives,
Its window frames and panes are twisted and broken.

But one can imagine the excitement the little girl
Must have felt when she finally reached
The building that held all of her dreams.
Of a future that she unknowingly would never attain.

She could not foresee that her world soon
Would be at war again and that a great Depression
Would tear her dreams and family apart.

Yet, for a brief snapshot in time,
The wonders of the world were inside the building
She was so excited to reach every morning.

Those few who pass by now are unfamiliar
With the joy that this one room school house provided.
They see it as just another building falling to the ground
On the back road of time.

But to me it signifies the roots of a genealogy
Which has been confronted by trials and tribulations
Ultimately finding redemption in the wonders of education.

May the dreams of the little girl always be remembered
As the seeds for a beautiful harvest
For all who come after.

# The Blue Spruce

Planted in love
Nourished by sweat
Your beauty is matched
Only by the sounds of the mellow clarinet.

From infancy you struggled
With the help of a friend
To inch toward the heavens limb by limb.
You stand as a guardian protecting your host
But you are not interested in fame or poetic boast.

Only that your presence be remembered when
He can no longer come again.

# The Ice Box

At a time when new appliances
Were thought to be a luxury
And beyond the family's budget,
They made do with an old
But functional – ice box.

It was used to insure that whatever meat
Could be secured
Would not rot.

Because the ice box was small and could not
Accommodate "extra meat",
They often turned to food from a can.
While a bit bland at times, it was tasty enough
Except for the occasional tin of Spam.

In times of food abundance now
It is hard to believe that there was something
Positive which was created out of those struggles.
But such was the case.

They constructed a weekly regime in the Winter
Out of necessity.
One which insured familial sustainability.

First, they loaded a few wooden crates with straw
On to the open bed of their old truck.
And then they secured next to the crates
A two man saw.
Then off to a family friend's pond they went.

Upon their arrival, they reached for shovels
To clear the snow which seemed to always
Fall over night.

Following their father's advice, they proceeded
To sledge hammer, chop, and saw
Blocks of ice.
They then carefully placed them in the straw lined crates.

They were on a mission
In an effort to please the Queen of the Kitchen.
And, on occasion, if they were lucky enough,
They returned home with the rewards of their
Ice fishing.

While their eventual purchase of a refrigerator
Made their lives much more conventional,
They lost a family ritual.

One wonders sometimes if they lost something important
In their move toward modernity.
But there remains doubt
That the Queen of the Kitchen would agree.

# Grammy's Clock

The stillness of the night is broken
By the soft whimpering of a child's cry.

It has begun again. The nightly loving exercise
Of parental response to their child's primordial need
For the comforting touch of another soul.

They try.

But the reassurances of Daddy or Mommy's embraces
Sometimes fail to calm the trembling emotion
Exploding from his tiny frame.

However, the answer to calm his fear
Is only steps away.

Sitting atop the antique bookshelf
Like an ancient oracle who possesses mystical powers
Of salvation is – Grammy's Clock.

Wound with delicate precision
She announces her presence on the half hour
And dutifully chimes the hourly passage of time.
Her rhythmic ticking fills the room with the comforting
Sound of her pendulum gently swaying back and forth.

Soon, accompanied with the sound of Daddy or Mommy's voice,
He finally surrenders to the reassurances that only
Grammy's Clock can provide.

"Tick, tock, tick, tock, tick, tock."

His fears have passed.
Grammy would be so pleased.

# His Time to Go

Much to do before he's done
The old man thought, as he peered
Through the frosty window.

The cows were still in the pasture below.
They needed to be brought back
To the barn and milked and removed from the falling snow.
But then he remembered that would be done
By his neighbor Joe.

He knew it was his time to go.
No longer would he be required to tend
The fire of his old stove.
No need to search for kindling under
The snow-covered limbs of the old pine.

He instinctively understood the signs.
No longer was his memory sharp.
He often forgot the simple tasks of the day.
Instead, he drifted into memories of children's laughter
As they played summers past.
But even those images didn't last.

Many friends had gone before.
Notices of their passing he had categorized
And placed in neat piles on the cabin floor.
No, not much more to accomplish.
He had tilled the land from dawn to dusk.
Made a living from his plow and sweat.
He asked nothing from friends or family
Except some unspoken respect.

He had no regrets, he thought.
Except for maybe one.
Did his philosophy of "sitting beside the road
And be a friend of all mankind" really produce
A similar action by those who passed by?
Did they even try? Oh well, did it really matter?

All that could be done has been finished.
Time to go.
He turned to the window – all that is left
Is to wait for Godot.

# An Australian Visitor

Shooting forth like gleaming comets
Across the night's sky
Are my thoughts in search for you.

Unending seeds of nothingness
Engulf my every emotion
Continually reminding me of the finality of the game.

Like a thief in the night you
Stole my love and then departed.
Return and finish what was started.

Find me once again hidden amongst the pages.
Rescue me from the superficiality of the roles
We were not meant to play.

# The Christmas Cactus

Nurtured by generations of family
Cautiously watered and sheltered
From light,
It stands as a yearly symbol of His everlasting might.

More than a lovely house plant
This loyal succulent became a friend.
Always with her,
Even to the end.

It provides a beautiful message to all left behind.
That life is fleeting and the importance
To be kind.
And that while our sorrow is deep
Our task is to always keep an understanding
Of the eternal cycle of the seasons.

Indeed, with its new buds already bursting with life,
It provides us with but one more reason
For hope and love.

Its friend would have wanted it that way.

# A Place in Time

Picking pieces of the past
Trying to create images which will last.
A feeble attempt to memorialize
The life of a man who tried
Time and again
To make sense of the tragedies placed
Before him
And yet provide for his family.

How to describe a man who meant so much to me?
No matter how difficult, it must be done.
He was my father. I was his son.

Similar to many men of his generation,
He did not seek formal education.
Instead reliance upon hard work and sweat
Would suffice, he thought.
All that was needed would be self-taught.

He courted and married a girl
From a family of seven children.
She shared his commitment to personal
Sacrifice. But dreamed of a future
Filled with possibilities – until she became sick.

She passed away too young. And the man succumbed
To the darkness that loneliness brings.
His old red truck which for years
Would carry his tools of ladders and brushes
No longer was a symbol of pride
Instead it reminded him of his lost bride.

The physical sacrifices of each day's labor
Seemed meaningless.
He became a man without a compass.

But regardless of his daily bouts of bitterness,
He retained a sense of pride in his memories
Of days past.
Of a stubborn little pony that he nurtured as a child
Of a model T car he bought to impress his girl
At a time in his life when his dreams
Were free and wild.
Of discussions at the old country store
Around a pot belly stove
Where he became the sage of all things
New and old.

But most of all, he filled his lonely nights
With thoughts of the girl
Who brought love and compassion
To a life filled with trials and tribulations.

# On To the Next Journey

Remembrances of family long past
Are chiseled into marble
All standing like soldiers in formation
Demanding attention and hoping that their time
On the Earth plane will be honored at last.

Scattered in unkept plots in the Mettowee Valley
With stones sometimes fallen to the ground
To manicured resting places in Dorset
Where other honored patriarchs and matriarchs
Of the Clan can be found.

Other proclamations carved into stone
Also withstand the passages of time
And can be seen
Across the Green Mountains
In a place called the Evergreen.

But there will be no such proclamation made for me.
No "perpetual care" stone declaring my time in space.

No, I respectfully prefer to be remembered, if at all,
By the call of a whipper will floating through
The branches of birches
Sitting atop Nichols Hill Road.

I know not who owns the little meadow
Which sits at the road's end.
But it is there that my Spirit will transcend
Time and space. It is the place where I can survey
The mountain where long ago
Two brothers built their homesteads
In hope to make their mark
On the little villages below.

It is the place where later generations of family gatherings
Would share their happiness and sorrows
Around an old rough cut maple log
That was made into a massive kitchen table.

It is there where memories of a little boy
Playing beside an old water trough
Filled with goldfish will be found.
Not a sacred plot with my bones placed under ground.

It is here where a new journey will begin.
Where my spirit will be set free
To frolic in the meadow and fly
With the wind. Up to the heavens
And back again.
To be embraced by the forest's canopy
For eternity.

# Waiting

I am waiting for the Moon to kiss
The night sky.

I am waiting for the sound of waves to embrace
The rocky shore line and to engulf the inlet
With the rhythm of the ocean
For ever more.

I am waiting for the sweet fragrance of the garden
To fill the air.
To send a message to the landscape and trees above
To not despair.

And to remind us all that as the circle turns
And our journeys seem to end
That life will return again
Regardless of the inhumanity of men.

I am waiting to rejoice again in the rising of a new Dawn
And in the knowledge that the children
Will frolic once again in the warmth of the midday Sun.
And that Love will once again conquer Hate.

I cannot wait.

# A Request

Yahweh, Elohim, Ohm, I have but one plea.
If I am granted it, forever shall I be in debt to thee.

Please help me keep my thoughts above
The storming tide which emaciates love.

Men of our century seem not to care
What history has taught us about warfare.
The killing, the hate, the inhumanity
And all the rest of its insanity
Can lead us all only to the conclusion
That men are truly a mere chemical solution.

But a powerful argument can be made
By those of us who have been waylaid
On a warm Spring night by the smell of a lilac
Or the rustle of a new maple leaf.

We know the key
Which separates men from beast.
All I ask is that my memory shall never cease.

# About the Author

Steven O. Ludd has deep roots in the soil of Vermont. The descendant of generations of farmers, a state Representative, and cheese makers, his passion for the people and the beauty of the Green Mountains is in full display in *Reflections Off the Lake*. So too is his commitment to the protection of democracy both in America and across the world. After receiving his law degree and doctorate from Syracuse University's College of Law and the Maxwell School of Citizenship and Public Affairs, he began a thirty year teaching career as a Professor of Constitutional Law at Bowling Green State University. Additionally, he served the United States Federal Court as both a Federal Court Monitor and as an Alternative Dispute Mediator and Arbitrator.

He presently resides in Saratoga Springs, New York with his wife Oksana Mihaychuk Ludd.

CPSIA information can be obtained
at www.ICGtesting.com
Printed in the USA
BVHW020134080922
646524BV00001B/2

9 781937 667290